## UNSEEN SCIENCE

# What Is the Color Spectrum?

Linda Ivancic

Cavendish Square

New York

Published in 2016 by Cavendish Square Publishing, LLC
243 5th Avenue, Suite 136, New York, NY 10016

Copyright © 2016 by Cavendish Square Publishing, LLC

First Edition

Website: cavendishsq.com

This publication represents the opinions and views of the author based on his or her personal experience, knowledge, and research. The information in this book serves as a general guide only. The author and publisher have used their best efforts in preparing this book and disclaim liability rising directly or indirectly from the use and application of this book.

CPSIA Compliance Information: Batch #CW16CSQ

All websites were available and accurate when this book was sent to press.

Library of Congress Cataloging-in-Publication Data

Ivancic, Linda, author.
What is the color spectrum? / Linda M. Ivancic.
pages cm – (Unseen science)
Includes index.
ISBN 978-1-5026-0921-2 (hardcover) ISBN 978-1-5026-0920-5 (paperback)
ISBN 978-1-5026-0922-9 (ebook)
1. Color–Juvenile literature. I. Title. II. Series: Unseen science.
QC495.5.I93 2016
535.6–dc23

2015023862

Editorial Director: David McNamara
Editor: Andrew Coddington
Copy Editor: Rebecca Rohan
Art Director: Jeffrey Talbot
Designer: Joseph Macri/Amy Greenan
Senior Production Manager: Jennifer Ryder-Talbot
Production Editor: Renni Johnson
Photo Research: J8 Media

Printed in the United States of America

# CONTENTS

# CHAPTER 1

# Take a Look

How beautiful the world around us is! Have you ever really considered all of the objects you can see? Take a look at everything around you. If you are outside, you may notice the sky, a sidewalk, a lawn, a car, or a neighbor taking a walk.

When inside, you might notice the fruit on the table, the poster on the wall, the computer screen, or the favorite socks covering your feet!

What is one thing that *all* these items have in common? Each of them has a particular color that we see when we look at it. Why is that? How come we don't see everything in the same color?

The world is filled with color! How many different colors do you see in these photos? Did you know that they all come from one source?

Why doesn't a color look the same when it's dark? Where do all these colors come from?

Let's go beyond what we can see and investigate the unseen science of color and the color **spectrum**.

## What Is Color?

In order to answer some questions, we may first need an understanding of other proven facts. To answer the question "What is color?" we need to talk about how color is described and how our eyes receive color information. To do that, we need to have an understanding of light.

## Light

The English scientist Isaac Newton discovered that light could be split into many colors by using a **prism**. A prism is a solid with a specific geometric shape, often made of glass with triangular ends. When sunlight passes through it, the light is bent to a different angle where we can see it separated into all the colors that make up the light. Sunlight isn't light of one color—it is made up of all the different colors mixed together. This color display is called a color spectrum.

A prism splits white light into its component colors. This color display is called the color spectrum.

Each visible color has a unique location and wavelength in the color spectrum.

A rainbow that forms after a rainstorm is a natural example of a prism. When sunlight passes through water droplets in the air at just the right angle, it bends different **wavelengths** within the light by different amounts. This causes the light to be displayed as separate colors.

Like the order of the letters in the alphabet, the order of colors does not change. The order of the color spectrum is red, orange, yellow, green, blue, indigo, and violet. An easy way to memorize the order is to remember the name of a nonexistent guy named "Roy G. Biv." Each letter in this name represents a color: *R* stands for red, *O* stands for orange, *Y* stands for yellow, *G* stands for green, *B* stands for blue, *I* stands for indigo, and *V* stands for violet.

Further study of the light spectrum shows that each color has a unique signature identifying its location and wavelength.

## Light As Waves

Light is a type of wave. It transfers energy and has wavelength and **frequency**. The colors we see are reflected light with certain wavelengths and frequencies. Not all light is color, though. There are other types of light, such as infrared light and X-rays, neither of which we can see. The **electromagnetic spectrum** helps us to visualize and study the characteristics of a wide range of light waves.

When we use the term "light," we mean a type of light wave that we can perceive with our eyes. We call these waves **visible light**. Visible light is a small region along the whole spectrum, with

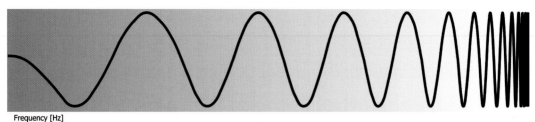

Frequency [Hz]

0  $10^2$  $10^4$  $10^6$  $10^8$  $10^{10}$  $10^{12}$  $10^{14}$  $10^{16}$  $10^{18}$  $10^{20}$  $10^{22}$  $10^{24}$

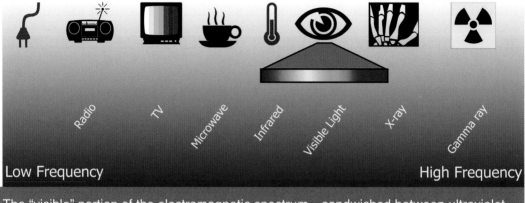

Radio   TV   Microwave   Infrared   Visible Light   X-ray   Gamma ray

Low Frequency                                    High Frequency

The "visible" portion of the electromagnetic spectrum—sandwiched between ultraviolet and infrared—represents the wavelengths of light that the human eye can detect.

the longest wavelengths of red being 700 **nanometers** (abbreviated nm) and violet having the shortest wavelength at around 400 nm.

## Don't Forget Roy G. Biv

Does a color's wavelength make a difference? It's interesting to note that in a rainbow, the shorter wavelengths of blue light are bent more than the longer wavelengths of red. That's why blue is always on the inside of a rainbow and red is on the outside.

While we might not see them, the light from the sun is a mix of many colors.

## This Chapter Has Shown

Light is important to our understanding of color. Light that we can see is called visible light. Visible light is only a small portion of the entire electromagnetic spectrum. Light has wave characteristics, and a color can be identified by its wavelength.

# CHAPTER 2

# What Color Is That?

olor is all around us. We have talked about color from an understanding of the visible light spectrum and that it is different wavelengths that create the different colors we see. What we see when we look at an object is reflected light. When light hits an object, some wavelengths are absorbed by that object—they are taken in and swallowed up like a sponge absorbs water—and some are reflected back to us. Let's do it— let's "make" color!

Filters can change the colors that we see.

# What Color Is That?

## Objective

To make color observations using color filters.

## Materials

- a piece of white paper
- a ruler
- a pencil
- four cotton swabs
- red, yellow, green, and blue food coloring
- a flashlight
- four clear plastic cups

## Procedure

1. Find a flat place to do the experiment, like a countertop, table, or desk. Cover the area with newspaper.

2. Place a few drops of blue food coloring on one end of a cotton swab.

3. Use the swab like a marker and make a blue dot about the size of a nickel (approximately 0.75 of an inch, or 2 centimeters, in diameter) on the white paper. Repeat this procedure with the red, green, and yellow food coloring. You should have one dot of each color on the paper.

Add a different color of dye to each cup of water.

It is important to record your results so that you can look back on them later.

4. Now, fill each cup halfway with water.

5. Add three to five drops of blue food coloring to one cup to create blue water. Do the same with the other three cups to create red, green, and yellow water. Mix with the matching color swab.

6. Turn on the flashlight and darken the room by shutting off the lights nearby or closing the curtains.

7. Hold the cup of red water directly above the red dot.

8. Shine the flashlight straight down into the cup of red water and look at the red dot. What color do you see? Write down your results on the chart. Tip: The recording chart on page 18 will help you keep track of the combinations to test.

9. Now look at the other three color dots through the cup of red water and record what you see.

10. Repeat the process with the other three cups of colored water and all four dots.

## Questions

- What did you find out about mixing color and light?
- Does it make any difference if you set the cup down or hold it above the dot?
- Do you get the same results for blue if you add more food coloring to make the water dark blue?

| Water Color | Dot Color | Color You See |
|---|---|---|
| Red | Red | |
| Red | Blue | |
| Red | Yellow | |
| Red | Green | |
| Blue | Red | |
| Blue | Blue | |
| Blue | Yellow | |
| Blue | Green | |
| Yellow | Red | |
| Yellow | Blue | |
| Yellow | Yellow | |
| Yellow | Green | |
| Green | Red | |
| Green | Blue | |
| Green | Yellow | |
| Green | Green | |

We can "twist" the perception of an object's true color by applying filters to what we see— such as when we wear sunglasses, use colored lighting, and apply makeup!

## Conclusion

You've just mixed different wavelengths together. When you are looking into the red water as it is held above a yellow dot, you see two wavelengths at the same time. The wavelengths for red and yellow combine, and you see orange. When red and blue mix, you see purple. Yellow and blue wavelengths mixed together make green.

# CHAPTER 3

# Color My World

I f visible light has all the ROYGBIV colors, how is it that the orange juice we drink is only orange in color?

## Reflection

An important wavelike behavior of light is **reflection**. When light hits an object, some of the ROYGBIV wavelengths are absorbed and some are reflected. The fruit of an orange reflects orange light and absorbs all the other light colors. That's also the case for the red paint on a fire truck, which reflects only the red part of light

The orange wavelength of light is reflected from the orange fruit; the green wavelength of light is reflected from the leaves.

but absorbs light of the other colors. Objects can be thought of as absorbing all the light wavelengths of colors except the color that our eyes observe.

## Refraction

Have you ever tried to run full speed into the ocean from the beach? The water slows you down, and you cannot run at that

same pace. Exactly the same thing happens to light when it goes from the air and shines into water, glass, or plastic. The light's speed slows down and the light waves bend. This is called **refraction**. We can see this by taking a glass of water and then placing a straw in the water. From the side, observe that the straw looks different above and below the water. Also notice how the straw looks like it "bends" where it enters the water.

## Black and White

Black and white are different from other colors. White is not a color at all. There is not a light wavelength that is characteristic of white. White is the combination of all the colors of the visible light spectrum. Sometimes, visible light is called "white light." A white daisy petal is reflecting all the color wavelengths of light back to us.

What happens to colored objects when you turn out the lights?

If a room has no windows and there is no light to reach our eyes, our eyes won't work—we need some amount of light to see an image. Of course, things in the room don't cease to exist! It's just that without reflected light, we can no longer see them.

In the light of day we do see things that appear black, like an asphalt road. The "black" here can be explained in that all the visible light is absorbed, and no light is reflected to our eyes. Technically speaking, black is just the absence of the wavelengths of the visible light spectrum.

## So Many Colors!

Colors can fall into different groups. One group is **primary colors**. These are the three colors that cannot be mixed or formed by any combination of other colors. All other colors are derived from these three **hues**, or colors. The primary colors are red, yellow,

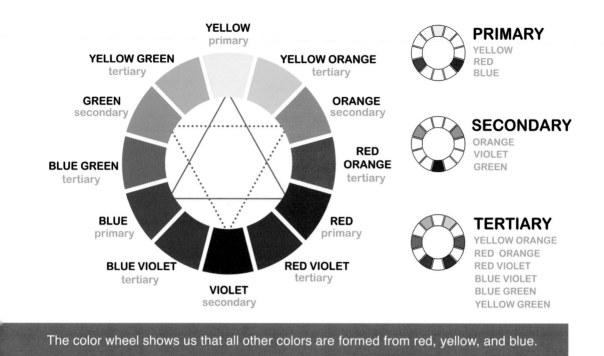

and blue. They can be arranged in a circle called the **color wheel**. When each of these three colors is mixed along their boundaries, the **secondary colors** are formed. The secondary colors are green, orange, and purple.

Each secondary color can be mixed with the primary color next to it on the wheel to form yet another two colors. These are called the **tertiary colors**. Each color is a two-word name, such as blue-green.

Wow, we only started with three colors and by the time we get to the third blending, we have twelve colors! Can you imagine

What Is the Color Spectrum?

We use different media to reproduce color, including color film, color paintings, color monitors, and color printers.

Nature is a master of color!

the potential color possibilities if we keep mixing? All these colors help to give our world its beauty!

## This Chapter Has Shown

Light and the colors we see with our eyes are affected by whether the light waves get pulled in (absorption), bounced back (reflection), or bent (refraction). Color theory shows that the primary colors of red, yellow, and blue are the origin of all other color formulation.

**color wheel** A circle with different-colored sections used to show the relationship between colors.

**electromagnetic spectrum** The entire range of electromagnetic radiation organized by wavelength and frequency. It includes radio waves, microwaves, infrared radiation, visible light, ultraviolet radiation, X-rays, and gamma rays.

**frequency** The number of times something is repeated, such as waves.

**hues** Shades or tints of colors.

**nanometer** A unit of distance in the metric scale, abbreviated as nm. One nanometer equals one thousand millionths of a meter (m) or 1 nm = 10-9 m (one billionth of a meter).

**primary colors** Colors that cannot be made from mixing other colors. Primary colors are the source of other colors. The primary colors are red, blue, and yellow.

**prism** A body that can be seen through, such as glass, whose ends are equal and parallel triangles, and whose three sides are parallelograms. Prisms are used for refracting or dispersing light.

**reflection** The return of light or sound waves from a surface without absorbing it.

**refraction** The turning or bending of any wave, such as a light or sound wave, when it passes from one medium into another of different optical density.

**secondary colors** Colors made by mixing two primary colors together: red and yellow make orange, yellow and blue make green, and red and blue make purple.

# GLOSSARY

**spectrum** The range of colors of wavelength energy sent out from a light source when viewed through a prism.

**tertiary colors** Colors resulting from the equal mixture of a primary color with either of the secondary colors adjacent to it on a color wheel.

**visible light** The part of the electromagnetic spectrum, between ultraviolet and infrared, that is visible to the human eye.

**wavelengths** Distances between two crests of a wave (or two troughs).

## Books

Jackson, Tom. *Experiments with Light and Color*. New York: Gareth Stevens, 2010.

Winterberg, Jenna. *Light and Its Effects*. Huntington Beach, CA: Teacher Created Materials, 2015.

Woodford, Chris. *Light: Investigating Visible and Invisible Electromagnetic Radiation*. New York: Rosen, 2012.

## Websites

**Introduction to the Electromagnetic Spectrum: The National Aeronautics and Space Administration (NASA)**
**science.hq.nasa.gov/kids/imagers/ems/**
Site developed for kids to explain the electromagnetic spectrum including radio waves, microwaves, infrared, visible, ultraviolet, X-rays, and gamma rays.

# FIND OUT MORE

**Light Science for Kids**

**www.explainthatstuff.com/light.html**

The "Explain That Stuff" site does just that! Written in easily understandable terms, the site explains the science workings of light and how that impacts our understanding of our world.

**Physics4kids.com: Types of Light**

**www.physics4kids.com/files/light_intro.html**

This site explores the nature of light—its energy, visibility, spectrum, and properties. This site also has additional reference materials and related links to take investigations further.

# INDEX

Page numbers in **boldface** are illustrations. Entries in **boldface** are glossary terms.

**Linda Ivancic**'s love for the natural world comes from her mother, who often told her to "Go outside and play!" She has spent twenty-eight years as an environmental, health, and safety consultant and has visited and explored many colorful places around the world, always learning something new. Motivated by her adult learners' "A-ha" moments when they grasp science in the world around them, she is committed to making science interesting and approachable to all age groups. Linda enjoys singing and "playing outside"; you will find her exploring on her bike, at the lake, and in the woods.